A SERIES IN

NATURE II

Also co-authored by Robert B. Warren:
Naked Spheres Of Ink
A Series In Nature

Order this book online at www.trafford.com
or email orders@trafford.com

Most Trafford titles are also available at major online book retailers.

bobwarrenphotography71@gmail.com

Printed in the United States of America.

ISBN: 978-1-4669-0279-4 (sc)

    978-1-4669-0278-7 (e)

Library of Congress Control Number: 2011960470

Trafford rev. 12/16/2011

Trafford
PUBLISHING®   www.trafford.com

North America & international
toll-free: 1 888 232 4444 (USA & Canada)
phone: 250 383 6864 ♦ fax: 812 355 4082

A SERIES IN
NATURE II

By
Robert B. Warren

Trafford Publishing
1663 Liberty Drive
Bloomington, In 47403

To my Family, Magdalena & Friends (including dogs and cats)

Everybody wants to go to Heaven but
Nobody wants to die
Everybody wants to know the reason
Without asking why
Phoebe Snow

There is a road, no simple highway between the dawn and the dark of night.
It is a road no one can follow. That road is for your steps alone.
The Grateful Dead

"First there is a Mountain then there is no Mountain then there is". Donovan

In memory of all who have gone before… including Shadow

Preface

Here are more photos from the same time period as the first: A Series In Nature.

This time I would like to elaborate on my perception of the concept of duality in nature.

In nature the concept of duality can be seen in its symmetry: from the molecular level in the blueprint of life: DNA's alpha-helical structure, and in the mirror image structures of organic chemicals called stereochemistry. All life is made of chemicals.

Even in the process's of life, cellular division we see symmetry in meiosis and mitosis.

There are basically two types of cells: diploid and haploid. The first are the cells that are the building blocks of all tissues and the second, haploid cells are the result of cellular division that produce the sex cells, eggs and sperm or pollen which combine to then produce diploid embryonic cells. The terms haploid and diploid refer to the number of identical copies of DNA, genes or chromosomes in every cell.

In the structures of vertebrates including ourselves we see bi-lateral symmetry. In invertebrates we do see Bi-lateral symmetry (ie.clam shells) but we see more radial symmetry (starfish, round worms, coral polyps and jellyfish).

How does duality or symmetry express itself in human consciousness? I believe it is seen in the expressions of the conscious and subconscious mind.

These ideas are spawned from my background in biology and psychology.

I hope you may find this interesting but I also hope you enjoy looking at these photographs which are just a reflection of the different wavelengths or colors of light seen in nature.

I have purposefully tried not to 'color enhance' any of these photographs.

Acknowledgements

Thanks to the medical community who devote their lives towards helping people.
And special thanks to Dr. Tom Cummings who saved and salvaged photos from Hawaii taken 40 years ago that I had thought were lost. In particular I am grateful to have the photo titled 'Night sky' shot at Polihale beach on Kauai- a time lapse photo taken in the middle of the night.

Contents

SPRING

Tulips

A Washington Ornamental

Washington ornamental

Washington flowers

Washington cherries

Orange red tulips

Orange & yellow tulips

Skagit valley tulips, WA

Budding leaves, CA

Budding leaves & flowers

Coalinga, CA

Northern CA

SUMMER

Puget sound, WA

Tidal zone, San Juan islands, WA

Primordial soup

In between the crack in the sidewalk

Forest undergrowth

Snoqualmie valley

Rosehips

FALL

Shadows

Leaves

Orange leaves

Yellow leaves

Red leaves

More orange leaves

Color & sky

Where a limb once grew

Tree trunk

Woodland park zoo

Lion

Skagit valley pumpkin field

Orange fungus

Salmon preparing to spawn

Mt. St .Helens after first eruption

LATE WINTER

Mt. Shasta

Zooming in

Small community, southern MT

Foothills of Rocky Mountains

Rocky Mt. Foothills

Hills, southern MT

Ranch land

ON THE ROAD

Horses, S. Utah

Horses & cow

E. side of Sierra Nevada's

Cows

Backside of Yosemite

E. CA Mountains

E. CA landscape

Landscape again

N. CA foothills

Foothills again

Leaning utility pole

California

Oak tree

Crossing over to NV

Ancient pine, dwarfed by harsh environment

Between CA & NV

N.W. AZ

Painting at Harris ranch, Coalinga, CA

IN THE AIR

Golden gate bridge

Antigua, Guatemala

Painting, Antigua, Guatemala

Gulf of Hondura's

Remembering

Beach flowers

Another Carribean sunset

HAWAII

Maui's W. coastline

Rocks at Makapu'u

Waikiki Aquarium

S.E. coast, Oahu

Porcupine fish

S.W. coast, Kauai

Hanalei Bay

Fern, Maui

Beach vine

Hibiscus

Foliage, Wailupe

Coconut trees

Tidal pool

Lava rock on hillside

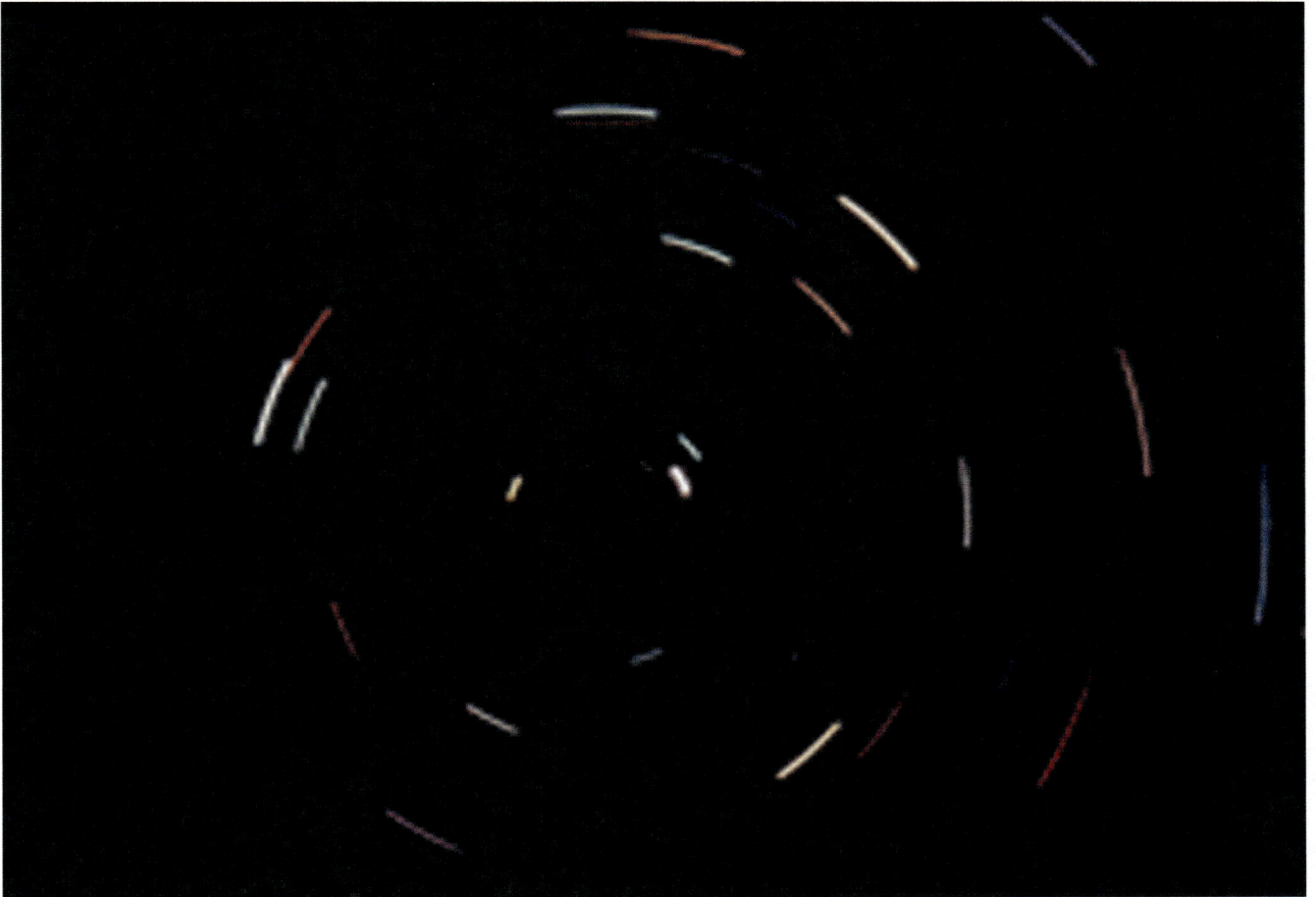

Night sky, Polihale Kauai

PACIFIC N.W. COAST

Near the coast

Washington State beach

Heceta lighthouse, OR

Seagulls, WA

Shorebirds

Coastal beach, OR

Watching the sunset, WA

ARIZONA

White Tank's

R.V. park, Phoenix

Bengal royalty

Poki

Zap & I

Made in the USA
Las Vegas, NV
08 June 2022